# Berkeley High School

# Berkeley High School

# Slang Dictionary

Communication Arts & Sciences
Berkeley High School

North Atlantic Books
Berkeley, California

Published by
North Atlantic Books
P.O. Box 12327
Berkeley, California 94712
Printed in Canada
Distributed to the book trade by Publishers Group West

Cover art by Eric Norberg
Illustrations by Nikkk Sonfield
and Lola Chenyek
Cover and book design by
Brooke Warner

*Berkeley High School Slang Dictionary* is sponsored by the Society for the Study of Native Arts and Sciences, a nonprofit educational corporation whose goals are to develop an educational and cross-cultural perspective linking various scientific, social, and artistic fields; to nurture a holistic view of arts, sciences, humanities, and healing; and to publish and distribute literature on the relationship of mind, body, and nature.

Library of Congress Cataloging-in-Publication Data
Berkeley High School slang dictionary / edited by Rick Ayers.
p. cm.
ISBN 1-55643-521-5 (pbk.)
1. English language—Dialects—California—Berkeley—
Dictionaries. 2. High school students—California—Berkeley—
Language—Dictionaries. 3. English language—California—
Berkeley—Slang—Dictionaries. 4. Americanisms—California—
Berkeley—Dictionaries. 5. Berkeley (Calif.)—Languages—
Dictionaries. I. Ayers, Rick. II. Berkeley High School (Berkeley,
Calif.)
 PE3101.C3B47 2004
 427'.949467--dc22
                      2004007152

1   2   3   4   5   6   7   8   TRANS   08   07   06   05   04

# Introduction

The reason that the students in Berkeley High School Communication Arts & Sciences (CAS) small school undertook to create this slang/vernacular dictionary is that we have been studying language, discourse communities, and word origins.

The idea of putting together the dictionary came up late and was only a small part of the linguistics unit we were doing. Even then, we only published it as something for the students in that class during the fall of 2000—the first run at the copy shop was 100 copies, for the students and the parents. I asked for a dollar per copy to cover costs. Somehow word got out. I think it was because Tom Dalzell, a Berkeley resident and renowned author of slang dictionaries, was given a copy by his neighbor, a Berkeley High student. Tom got in touch with the *San Francisco Chronicle* as well as the

Oxford English Dictionary office of vernacular. Before we knew it, we were a phenomenon. Articles appeared in the newspaper, followed by television stories. These would inspire new written stories and then new television stories. Pretty soon, we were getting books printed in lots of 100 and charging $5 instead of $1 to the people who were finding us on the web and asking us for a copy.

We began to update the dictionary every spring, something of a class project, again embedded in the unit on linguistics. I was uncertain how the dictionary would be received by many different sectors. Would we be chastised for undermining the teaching of "proper" English? Would we look like we were manipulating or using the youth voice? Finally, I sent a copy to Lisa Delpit, the foremost expert on issues of language and power (see the reference to her two books at the end of this introduction). I was delighted to get back a note from her:

> Dear Rick, Thanks so much for sending me the Slang Dictionary. I really enjoyed reading the entries and delighted in the choices the kids made. What an absolutely wonderful learning experience. Teachers labor so hard over "parts of speech"—if they did something like this, it would be so much easier! ... p.s. Maya [her daughter] was fascinated w/ the dictionary.

At that point, I realized we were onto something. My only concern with the media coverage was that

I did not want the kind of "other" stories about the cute and/or dangerous young people and the odd ways they spoke. If the stories could reflect some sense of the wisdom and depth these students have, we would let them come. Just after we thought the frenzy had died down, back-to-school would come up and another reporter would remember the dictionary and run a piece on it, starting the cycle of media coverage again. This coverage went as far as NPR's radio quiz show, "Wait Wait … Don't Tell Me!," the CBS morning news, and CNN. Finally, we were approached by Richard Grossinger of North Atlantic Books here in Berkeley. We agreed to sign a contract and to turn over the handling of printing and distribution to them. All the funds from the dictionary (about a buck a book) were to go to the CAS program—to further the learning opportunities for students.

Once the book was in the hands of professionals, sales really took off. In spring of 2004, we found ourselves third on the East Bay best-seller list according to the *East Bay Express* and then on the *San Francisco Chronicle* best-seller list for the Bay Area three weeks in a row. We have now updated the book with over fifty new entries and deleted about ten words that no longer fit. And we are poised for national distribution. All this from a little class project!

In spite of the efforts of dictionary makers to freeze language at a particular moment and to prescribe the proper spelling and definition of words, language is always a dynamic, changing, exciting world—as exciting as the human cultures it represents.

When my daughter, who graduated from Berkeley High in 1999, went off to college in Oregon, she found that her language contained some words that were unique to California and some that were even unique to Berkeley. The mixing of young people from different high schools made them all suddenly aware of the complexity of language. The *Berkeley High School Slang Dictionary* will be an ongoing project—perhaps managing to freeze a few moments in time for a future researcher to discover.

Standard English, after all, is only the distillation of a certified version of the language. Of the many tribes and sectors that vied for power in early Anglo-Saxon-Norman Britain, one blending came out on top and declared their language the standard. It is often said, "The standard language is the dialect with the strongest army." But even when the standard is established, the most creative and wonderful part of the language is the way it continues to change.

Shakespeare, of course, is said to have "originated" thousands of words, or at least to be the one who first wrote them down. Today we think of The Bard as the ultimate in "high English," the standard, the most educated. But what made him great was his endless curiosity, his great ear for the spoken word. Unlike the scholastic playwrights of the age, who were university educated and only used "proper" English, Shakespeare never made it to college. Shakespeare was familiar with the many dialects of English—the different constructions and words in Surrey, Kent, High Country Northumberland, as well as various working-class brogues and variations. His art was his inventiveness, his ear for the genuine, and his willingness to cross borders.

Word definitions and grammar rules are wonderful resources and important to know. But they should only serve to help us get language rather than limiting and placing borders on its inventiveness. More, I suggest that the most creative front of language, the place where new inventions are constantly taking place, is in the marginalized communities, the underclass of society. Most of the new words entering American English—like most of the new music in America—comes from the African American community and the African American experience. We also have the blending of different languages— many American high schools have students who speak dozens of languages between them. Then there is the youth culture as a whole, with all of its diversity. Yes, technology has also brought us many new words—email language is now entering the dictionaries—but it runs a distant second to the contributions of communities on the margins of official, standard English.

This has been true throughout history. Jerry Badanes argues that the creative side of German in the '20s and '30s was within the Jewish community. It was there that new words were invented, that Eastern and Western influences bent the language, that German sang with a vibrancy. With the Holocaust, and with the elimination of Jews from German cultural life, the German language stagnated.

There is a long history of writing in vernacular and studying vernacular. This is not only true in Europe (the flourishing of Yiddish literature, for example) but especially in the democratic United States. Martin Delaney was one of the first African American authors to write extensively in vernacular—in the 1850s. During the Harlem Renaissance, Paul Laurence Dunbar and Zora Neale Hurston celebrated the creativity of African American language in the United States.

We have undertaken this study of language not to heap contempt on what is known as standard English (though I hate to hear people call it "proper English"). Rather, we are interested in investigating all the discourse communities we encounter. It is important for students in high school to develop a metacognition about their language skills, to be able to think about what they are doing, and to appreciate their strengths. As students think about their own language usage, they can also think about what goes into the "standard" forms of our society. The important thing is not to reject one or the other but to recognize the importance of the skill of "code switching," to change styles between youth vernacular and standard English in order to communicate, depending on the situation. Awareness of audience—the ability to know which form to use in which situation—is the mark of a good writer and speaker.

Some educators have been doing these kinds of studies of youth language for years. Connie Elbe at the University of North Carolina has had her students collect slang words and phrases since the early '70s. See her book, *Slang and Sociability* (New York, London: University of North Carolina Press, 1996). We can access extensive resources on slang and vernacular on the Internet on sites such as www.anthonyvitti.com/hiphopdictionary and www.rapdict.org.

During this process of studying vernacular speech and slang, CAS students have tried writing down overheard conversations in order to pay attention to the inventions and creations of the daily oral language of their peers. CAS students have also written pieces in vernacular then translated them to standard English. And each student has turned in cards with at least three current slang words, paying attention to the pronunciation, the part of speech, the definition, the sample sentence, and any information that can be gathered on the word roots, the etymology.

While hip hop and African American culture predominated in the collected list, including those from white students, there were also words that came from Chicano, Jewish, Hindi, punk, and sports cultures. We left out other inventive areas of youth language, such as pager code, which has gone out of style with the advent of the cell phone. Every teenager used to know the warm feeling of getting 143 (I love you) on a pager as well as the cold fear provoked by 187 (police code for homicide).

For the current dictionary we have also drawn on the work of Phil Halpern's Berkeley High English classes, some in the Computer Academy and some in the regular school, which have compiled slang dictionaries for a number of years. We have consulted this work to fill out any words or phrases we have overlooked that might be helpful. We have also consulted current and classic slang dictionaries to be reminded of ones we might have missed. The drafts of this dictionary have drifted around many classrooms, with students adding annotations, corrections, and new words.

Of course, students think it strange to be the objects of a kind of cultural anthropology. They laugh when I interrupt a conversation to ask them to repeat a word and to explain its exact meaning. After all, I am an adult invading their cultural space, attempting to decode that which has been encoded precisely to make it their own. Sometimes my curiosity has been humored, sometimes it has been annoying. Certainly, this class has created an interesting reversal of power relationships: after all, they are the experts on these words, I am the one who does not know, who needs guidance. Sometimes the way their words look on the page, the way they are defined by the slang dictionary, seems imprecise and wrong. This is the same experience any people have when they are the subject of anthropological study.

It is, nevertheless, worthwhile to draw some conclusions about the "youth culture" of Berkeley High School by looking at the frequency of appearance of different words. Young people invent new words for things that are not adequately described by the standard vocabulary or for concepts that matter to them and are the object of humor and invention.

Paolo Freire, the great Brazilian educator and revolutionary talks about the ways to go about teaching literacy to the oppressed. His fundamental point is that education and literacy are a matter of power. When he is teaching those at the bottom of society he does not simply attempt to deliver them to the language of privilege, of empire, of the ruling class. Instead he helps them name their own world, he allows them to make personal dictionaries of words that have meaning to them, sometimes dangerous words like "land reform" and "self-determination," as well as "love" and "passion." His fundamental point is that by naming the world the oppressed begin to have power over it. That's how important words are. By accident we stumbled upon a Freirian educational model, one that found our students as engaged and interested and caring as the Brazilian peasants in their literacy campaign forty years ago.

I previously wrote about the many names the Inuit

(Eskimo) people have for snow and how that reflects the way language bends to describe different realities. But I was corrected—the snow story is apocryphal, though it seemed so right it is hard to let go of. While there may indeed be only one or two Inuit words for snow, the language they use to describe the various states of winter weather is certainly rich and complex. Similarly, in Peru the people use the term *garua* to describe a kind of misty rain that occurs in the mountains—something not seen in other climates. The point here is that we can deduce certain values of today's teens from words in the slang dictionary.

Young people in the U.S. and in Berkeley have plenty of words for marijuana and the consumption of marijuana. You'll find in this dictionary such words as endoe, chronic, dojah, mota, gooey balls, blunts, joints, bogart, ganja, blessed sacrament, bomb, pookie, pinner, shake, bud, and bammer. Perhaps because these words are supposed to keep the conversation away from the ears of adults, new ones are constantly invented. Such terms as gage, grefa, juja, and bhang made it into the slang dictionary two years ago but are mostly out of use now. But, thank goodness, the many words of the heroin and cocaine subculture are rare here. Perhaps as a result of drugs in youth culture, there are also many words for the police—po-po, five-0, rollers, and heat.

Sad to say, there are many words in today's youth culture for steal: chalk, gaffle, gank, jank, break. And there are plenty of words that reflect teenage interest in clothing: fit, fitted, rathead, booty, clean. We can worry about the degradation of personal relations and sexuality with such impersonal words for sex as hit and poke. We know there are degrading names for women, gay people, and every race and ethnic group. Most of these did not make it into the dictionary because no one saw fit to submit them, except for some words that are so common that they must be listed and perhaps discussed in a "usage note."

Teenagers today are loyal and caring about their peers. Many words for pride and respect pop up, such as represent and props. And perhaps the largest group of words exists for friend, lovers, and groups of friends: home, homey, folks, G, OG, clique (and the Spanish cliqua), set, dude, cousin, nizzel, boo, whoady, blood, patna, peeps, crew, bro', brougham, and money.

For the purpose of this dictionary, we have limited the parts of speech to noun, verb, adverb, interjection, and verb forms. Sometimes a word will come into the dictionary that is really a verb form used another way. Usually that is a word ending in "-ed" (e.g. gaffled), which can act as an adjective or a past participle; or one ending in "-ing" (e.g. cheesin'), which can be an adjective or a present participle.

A word on etymology. We included the word histories to the best of our knowledge, sometimes consulting other sources, sometimes relying on peer knowledge. In the earlier editions, we called the word history "etymology" at the end of the entry. A number of readers have pointed out that we were not giving the thorough history of the origin of a word. For this reason, we changed the word choice to "origin" to reflect the place or time of entry point of a word into teen slang. For example, the word "scraper" is a current name for a certain type of Detroit car. Instead of going back to the Old Norse and Middle English origin of "scrape," we simply reference the African American culture as the origin in this issue.

This dictionary has now become an ongoing project. Please feel free to submit new words for the 2006 edition. All comments, critiques, and submissions can be submitted to me at rayers@berkeley.k12.ca.us.

—Rick Ayers

The main resources that were consulted in the creation of this dictionary (for missing words and sometimes for etymology) were:

*American Heritage Dictionary* (Boston: Houghton Mifflin,1992).

Dalzell, Tom. *Flappers 2 Rappers: American Youth Slang* (Springfield: Mirriam-Webster, 1996).

Delpit, Lisa, and Joanne Dowdy, Eds. *The Skin That We Speak: Thoughts on Language and Culture in the Classroom* (New York: New Press, 2002).

Dunn, Jerry. *Idiom Savant: Slang as it is Slung* (New York: Henry Holt, 1997).

Major, Clarence. *Juba to Jive: A Dictionary of African-American Slang* (New York: Penguin Books, 1994).

Perry and Delpit. *The Real Ebonics Debate* (Boston: Beacon Press, 1998).

Walter and Skeat. *Etymological Dictionary of the English Language* (Oxford: Clarendon Press, 1963).

**A'ight** (ah-ITE) *adj.,* OK, good, fine. From "all right." "I'll be down in a minute, a'ight." [*Origin,* African American]

**Agarro, se la agarro** (say la ah-GAR-o) *v.,* To hit, punch, fight someone. "She was mad y se la agarro." [*Origin,* Chicano/Spanish]

**Ancient** (AYN-shent) *adj.,* Old, out of style. "Your fit is ancient." [*Origin,* Hip hop]

**Ankle biters** (ang-kel bye-ters) *n.,* Little kids. "I had to babysit last night, a pair of ankle biters."

**Apple bottom** (AP-pul BOT-um) *n.,* Round-shaped buttocks that look like two round apples. Also, the name of Nelly's jean company. "God must love me to have sent a girl with an apple bottom into my life." See Cake. [*Origin,* youth culture]

**Area code** (air-e-ah code) *n.,* Location of a place by the telephone area code. "I'm going to head over to the 510." [*Origin,* Nate Dogg]

**-ass** (ass) *suffix/adj.,* Adds emphasis to an adjective. "Those are some good-ass cookies." "That is a bad-ass haircut."

**Babylonian** (bab-i-LOW-nee-an) *n.,* A white or Caucasian person. "I don't like to eat when the cook is Babylonian." [*Origin,* Rastafarian, from Old Testament biblical, the Babylonians were the people who enslaved the Israelites]

**Baked** (baykt) *adj.,* Under the influence of marijuana. "I could tell he was half-baked but the rest of them were hella baked." [*Origin,* Drug subculture]

**Baller** (BALL-er) *n.,* A highly praised and respected individual, someone who has a lot of money; someone who plays basketball well. "The class of '02 is full of ballers." [*Origin,* African American]

**Bammer** (BAM-ur) *n.,* Marijuana that is weak, of low potency. "Hey, is all you have is bammer?" [*Origin,* Drug subculture] See: Shake

**Bank** (bank) *n.,* Money. "She had hella bank in her wallet." Also: **Bank roll,** a lot of money. Also: **Bank,** *v.,* To punch. "He was getting' banked on." [*Origin,* African American]

bank

**Baseball** (BASE-bal) *n., v., adj.,* An answer to any question, having no relation to the question. "What is 2 x 2?" "Baseball." [*Origin,* '90s Berkeley]

**Benjamin** (ben-je-min) *n.,* A hundred dollar bill. "That armored car busted open and hella Benjamins blew out."

**Biotch** (BEE-ach) *n.,* Derogatory word for woman or person, from "bitch," female dog. "02, like what, biotch." [*Origin,* Hip hop] *Usage note:* While biotch is widely used by males and females, this term, along with "bitch," is a reflection of negative cultural values, contempt for women, and in some cases violence against women. It is found in much popular music.

**Blessed sacrament** (BLES-id SAK-ri-ment) *n.,* Marijuana, *bot.,* cannabis sativa. "It's time to take out the blessed sacrament." [*Origin,* Rastafarian]

**Bling bling** (bling bling) *interj.,* Shiny, sparkling with jewels or gold, good. "That ring is fly, bling bling." [*Origin,* Hip hop]

**Blood** (blud) *n.,* Friend, person of the same race, family member. "Yo, blood, I'll see you tomorrow." [*Origin,* from blood brother, '60s Black Nationalist.]

bling bling

**Blown up** (blone up) *v.*, To get paged excessively. "Ten people have paged her in five minutes; she is getting blown up." Also: When pager is going off. "Hey, you're blowin' up!" [*Origin*, African American]

**Blown-up** (blone-up) *adj.*, To be well-known. "After that shutout, Herman was blown-up at the school."

blown up

**Blunt** (blunt) *n.*, A large marijuana cigarette, or cigar. "He rolled a big blunt." [*Origin*, Phillie Blunts are a type of cigar which are often purchased, the tobacco removed, and large quantities of marijuana are inserted.]

**Bogart** (BOW-gard) *v.*, To hoard, hog, or monopolize, especially a marijuana cigarette. "Don't bogart that joint, my friend." [*Origin*, Humphrey Bogart constantly had a cigarette in his mouth.]

**Bomb** (bahm) *n.*, Marijuana, *bot.* cannabis sativa. "Hey, let's smoke some bomb." [*Origin*, Drug subculture] Also: Something good, excellent, superlative. "That's the bomb." Also: *v.*, To erect a graffiti display, to paint a wall. "We bombed that train station!" [*Origin*, From *Bomb the Suburbs*, by William Upski Wimsatt]

**Boo/boo boo** (boo) *n.*, Pet
name for your signifi-
cant other. "Come on
over and sit with me,
boo." [*Origin,* Hip hop]
**Boo boo** (boo boo) *adj.*,
Bad, weak. "How you
like that new Jetta."
"Aw, Jettas is boo boo,
dog."
**Bootsy** (BOOT-see) *adj.*,

boo

Bad, negative, hateful.
"Man, I can't believe you did that to me, that's hella
bootsy." [*Origin,* Hip hop]
**Booty** (BOOT-ee) *adj.*, Bad, especially ugly or badly
dressed. "He looks booty." Also: The human buttocks, as in "booty call." Also: **Booty huggers,** overly
tight-fitting pants "That girl was wearing such tight
booty huggers that she couldn't even bend down."
[*Origin,* African American]
**Bounce** (bauns) *v.*, To leave an area, vacate, go away,
spring back. "Hey, patna, let's bounce from the spot."
[*Origin,* African American]
**Bourghetto** (boo-JHET-oh) *adj.*, Combination word
made from bourgeois and ghetto. Described by Barry
Ronge of *South African Sunday Times* (12/3/2003)
as "rich, middle-class African American hipsters who
cling to street style and street music, affecting the

pose of the ghetto, while they are living an 'Oreo-cookie' Park Avenue lifestyle." [*Origin*, Bloggers, also Rap stars Nelly and Ali]

**Break** (brak) *v. refl.,* To give up, surrender, as in cash or jewelry. "Break yourself for those stones." [*Origin*, Hip hop]

**Breezy** (BREE-zi) *n.,* Young woman. "What's up with you and that breezy." [*Origin*, African American]

breezy

**Bro'** (broe) *n.,* Brother, friend. "I'll catch you later, bro'. Also: **Brougham,** (BRO-ham), brother, high class person, named after model of Cadillac. [*Origin*, African American]

**Bubblatin'** (BUB-el-ay-ten) *pres. part.,* Relaxing, hanging out, chilling with friends. "We weren't causing any problem. We were just bubblatin'." [*Origin*, '90s youth culture]

**Bud** (bud) *n.,* The best part of the marijuana plant, where most of the oils and drug are concentrated. A word for marijuana, *bot.,* cannabis sativa. "Hey, you have some great bud there." [*Origin*, Drug subculture]

**Buggin'** (buggin) *v.,* Worrying. "Why are you buggin'? You know she likes you." [*Origin*, African American]

**Bum out** (bum aut) *n.,* Someone who is depressed, a

loser, washed up, a stoner. "That guy is such a bum out." [*Origin,* Punk rock]

**Bummer** (bummer) *n.,* A disappointment; unfortunate thing. "I'm sorry to hear about your new car, that's a real bummer." [*Origin,* Hippie culture, '60s]

**Bum-rush** (bum rush) *v.,* To invade, slam, sometimes unexpectedly "We bum-rushed him from the side." [*Origin,* African American]

**Burn** (buhrn) *v., (pres. part.,* **burnin'**) Someone who has unprotected sex and now has a sexually transmitted disease. "That girl was a rippa and now she burnin'!"

**Buster** (BUS-ter) *n.,* Someone who is foolish or disliked. "The president is a buster." [*Origin,* Punk rock]

**Cake** (CAK) *n.,* Well-shaped body, especially thighs and butt. "Damn, girl, that aerobics instructor Darryl got cake!"

**Cap** (cap) *n.,* Bullet. "I'm gonna bust a cap in his ass."

**Cethas** (SEETH is) *n.,* Mother, mama from a shortened and mispronounced adaptation of "mamacita." That is, Spanish speakers in New York say "cita" as short for mamacita and non-Spanish speakers have picked it up and altered it to cethas. On cethas means "on mama," which means extremely important, serious. "You'd better get out of my face right now, and I put that on cethas." [*Origin,* New York, Puerto Rican]

**Chalk** (chalk) *v., (past part.,* **chalked**) Steal. "Someone chalked my boom box." [*Origin,* '90s youth culture]

**Check** (chek) *v.,* To pay attention to, to be aware of. Especially used as reflexive verb, as in, "Watch it, bro', you'd better check yourself." [*Origin,* African American]

**Cheddar** (ched-er) *n.,* Money. "I'm all about my cheddar."

**Cheese** (cheez) *v., (pres. part.,* **cheesin'**) Smile. "Emilia must have finally hooked up, look how she's cheesin'" [*Origin,* '90s youth culture]

**Chill** (chil) *v.,* To relax, hang out, spend time casually. "I'm just going to chill at home." *Pres. participle:* chillin'. [*Origin,* African American]

**Cholo (Chola)** (cho-lo) *n.,* A Chicano, born in the U.S. "That cholo has a fine fit, eh?"[*Origin,* Chicano/Spanish]

**Chop it up** (chop it up) *v. clause,* Talking, talking with friends with great interest, enthusiasm.

chill

"Girl, last night we were choppin' it up." [*Origin,* '90s youth culture]

**Chorba** (CHOR-bah) *n.,* Girlfriend, somebody's woman friend, one's woman. "Don't mess with my chorba." [*Origin,* Mountains of northern Spain]

**Chronic** (KRAN-ik) *n.,* Marijuana, *bot.* cannabis sativa. "He's messed up because he can't lay off the chronic." [*Origin,* Rastafarian]

**Chunk** (chunk) *v.,* To fight "If they keep bothering us, we're going to chunk 'em" [*Origin,* '90s youth culture]

**Clean** (cleen) *adj.,* Looking good in a neat way. "That outfit was clean." [*Origin,* African American]

**Cliqua** (KLEE-ka) *n.,* Also: **Clika.** A group of friends. "We're going to let her hang out with our cliqua this weekend." [*Origin,* Spanglish, mixture of Spanish and English, and Chicano]

**Clique** (clik) *n.,* Also: **Click.** A group of friends. "We're going to let her hang out with our click this weekend." [*Origin,* '60s youth culture]

**Clown** (klown) *v., n.,* Make fun of, act

clique

crazy; a fool. "It was cold of you to clown on Jesse."
[*Origin,* African American]

**C-note** (SEE note) *n.,* A hundred dollars. "He owe me
a C-note and if he don't pay, I'ma scrape him." [*Origin,* from the Roman numeral "C" for 100, abbrevi-
ation for Centum]

**Coin** (koyn) *n.,* Money, a metal used for money. "Hey,
man, you got some coin on those fries?" [*Origin,*
African American]

**Cold** (cold) *adj.,* Mean, evil, cold-hearted, not nice. "It
was real cold of Bo to make fun of his friend." [*Origin,* African American]

**Conniption** (con-NIP-shun) *n.,* A fit of violent emotion,
such as anger or panic. Also: **Conniption fit.** "Hey,
mom, don't have a conniption fit." [*Origin,* '50s middle America]

**Cop** (cawp) *v.,* To get, to acquire. "I'm going to cop that
new Jay Z CD."

**Crew** (cru) *n.,* A group
of friends. "We're
going to let him
hang out with our
crew this weekend."
[*Origin,* '90s youth
culture]

**Crib** (krib) *n.,* Home,
house, apartment,
bedroom. "I've been

crew

lyin' up at the crib all day." [*Origin*, '40s, Jazz, African American]

**Crotch Walker** (kroch WOK-er) *n.*, Shoplifter. "Fool, I'm the best crotch walker in town." [*Origin*, Berkeley]

**Crucial** (KRU-shell) *adj.*, Excellent, the best, fantastic. "That film was crucial." [*Origin*, '90s Chicago youth culture]

**Crunk** (krunc) *v.*, (*past part.*, **crunked**) Loud or intoxicated. "That stuff got me hella crunked."

**Crusty** (KRUS-tee) *adj.*, Messed up, dirty, old. "I couldn't stand sitting next to that crusty man in the theater." [*Origin*, '90s youth culture]

**Cup-cakin'** (cup-CAK-en) *v.*, When a girl and boy are always together, kissing and hugging up. "Girl, I seen you and him been cup-cakin in the hallway every morning."

**Cuts** (kutz) *n.*, Far away, located far from the rest of the city. "We had to drive to the cuts to pick up my friend." [*Origin*, African American]

**Cuzin, Cuz** (CU-zin, cuz) *n.*, A friend or associate. "What's up, Cuz?" [*Origin*, African American]

cup-cakin'

**Dank** (dank) *n.,* Marijuana, *bot.* cannabis sativa. "Let's smoke some dank." [*Origin,* Drug subculture]

**Dawg** (dawg) *n.,* Friend, partner. A grown man; one with experience. "Hey, I'll catch you later, dawg." [*Origin,* Hip hop]

**Dead Presidents** (ded PRES-i-dents) *n.,* Money, cash. "Friday's pay day. I'll finally have my dead presidents." [*Origin:* The pictures on U.S. currency are of former presidents, African American]

**Dealio** (DEE-lee-oh) *n.,* The deal, the situation. "Hey, y'all, what's the dealio around here?" Ending put on simply for aural effect. This trend seems to have started after the rapper Coolio started putting out music. See: foolio.

**Deez-nuts** (deez nutz) *n.,* Literally, these testicles. Used to refer to oneself. "I'm not going to let anyone mess with deez-nuts." Also: Negative response to a question. "Hey, pass that joint." "Deez-nuts." **Nuts** is also used to mean "leave me alone," in "Get off my nuts." [*Origin,* Hip hop]

**Dick head** (dik hed) *n.,* A stupid person, idiot. "Man, he is such a dick head." [*Origin,* '70s youth culture]

**Dill Piece** (dil pees) *n.,* Male genitals. "He can't think of anything but his dill piece." [*Origin*, '90s youth culture]

**Dime** (dyem) *n.*, A girl who looks so good she's a perfect ten. "Did you see that girl at the party last night? She was a total dime piece."

**Dirty** (DER-tee) *adj.*, Badly dressed, wearing old clothes. "She looks dirty, look at her pants." Also: Refers to someone who is sexually promiscuous. [*Origin*, '90s youth culture]

**Dis** (dis) *v.*, Shortened version of "disrespect." "Hey, Mr. Irving, don't be dissin' me."

**Dojah** (DOE-jah) *n.*, Marijuana, *bot.* cannabis sativa. "All he ever thinks about is the old dojah." [*Origin*, Drug subculture]

**Donut** (DOE-nut) *n.*, A circular mark left by tires of a car that has spun in a short circle. "He was doin' donuts at the intersection." [*Origin*, '90s youth culture]

**Down with** (down with) *prep.*, In agreement with, used when something sounds good to the speaker. "Want to go to Ben and Jerry's?" "I'm down with that!"

**Down-low** (down lo) *adj.*, Also: **d.l.** Secret, private, not made public. "Let's just keep it on the down-low." Or: "Let's just keep it on the d.l." [Origin, '90s youth culture]

down-low

**Drama** (DRA-mah) *n.*, Major preoccupation, concern, obsession. "There is all kinds of drama with him about his parents." [*Origin*, '90s youth culture]

**Dubs** (dubz) *n.*, Twenty, pertaining to twenty dollars. "My car rides on dubs." [*Origin*, '90s youth culture]

**Dude** (dood) *n.*, A man, friend. Someone fastidious in dress and manner. "Hey, dude, let's get going." *v.*, To dress up. "I am going to get duded up." [*Origin*, '70s youth]

endoe

**Ear Hustlin'** (eer HUS-ling) *v. pres. part.*, Eavesdropping, listening on to conversation. "Tell your sista to stop ear hustlin' when I talk to you on the phone."

**Edumacation** (ED-you-ma-KAY-shun) *n.*, Education. Used in self-deprecating reference to getting an education. When it is said with purposeful mispronunciation, it suggests that the student isn't learning anything. "I'm not going to hang out in the park all day. I have to drop by school and get my edumacation on." [*Origin*, '80s youth]

**Endoe** (EN-doe) *n.*, Marijuana, *bot.* cannabis sativa. "I'm trying to find some endoe." [*Origin*, Rastafarian]

**Ese** (ES-ay) *pron.*, Literally, "that," but used as: You, brother, friend, comrade. "Wazzup, ese?" [*Origin*, Chicano/Spanish]

**Ethyl** (EH thil) *n.*, The highest valued thing. "On ethyl" means "On everything that I love." "I'm telling the truth, and I put that on ethyl." [*Origin*, African American]

**Extended food privileges** (ex-TEN-did fud PRI-vi-le-jus) *n.*, Getting on the good side of a friend and being rewarded with food. "I got extended food privileges at Tom's house." [*Origin*, '90s youth culture]

**Fa Sho** (fah SHOW) *exclam.*, Yes or thank you. "Do you want to go the the Super Bowl?" "Fa Sho!"

**Fade** (fad) *v.*, To pay for part of something in order to get a part of it. "That looks like a good pie, can I fade on that?" Also: To slip away, disappear. "When the cops roll up, you have to fade." Also: Used to mean drunk, "He was hella faded last night." When used as *noun*, a haircut, especially in African American males, in which the hair is beveled in to the skin. "Hey, man, did you see my fade?" [*Origin*, African American]

**Fat** (fat) *adj.*, Large, good, excellent. "I had a fat load of homework last night." "That was such a fat song, man!" Also: *adv.*, **Fatly.** See: Phat. [*Origin*, African American]

**Feel me** (feel me) *v.*, To be in agreement with. "The teacher is being hypocritical, do you feel me?" [*Origin*, African American]

fat

**Firme** (FEER-may) *adj.,*
Strong, solid, loyal. "You're
my firme bro, bro." [*Origin,*
from Spanish, Chicano]
**Fit** (fit) *adj.,* Also: **Fitted.**
Fashionably dressed, well
dressed, wearing current
styles. ("He is really fitted.")
[*Origin,* African American]
**Five-0** (five oh) *n.,* The police.
"Watch it, man, five-0 on
that side street." The term
5-0 became slang when the
show "Hawaii 5-0" was
popular. The use of "5-0"

five-o

referred to the fact that Hawaii is the fiftieth state.
The word was divided by a hyphen, however, because
it referred to the police program. [*Origin,* police code
for police officers]
**Flossy** (FLOSS-ee) *adj.,* Cool, clean, excellent. "That's
a flossy-ass car." [*Origin,* '90s youth culture]
**Fly** (flie) *adj.,* Beautiful, clean, honorable. "That guy is
so fly." "She's so fly." [*Origin,* 19th-century England,
stylish coach]
**Fo' Sheazy** (fo SHEE-zee) *adj.,* Also: **Fo' shizzel.** For
sure, emphatic positive expression, certainly, positive acknowledgement. "Do you want to go with
her?" "Fo' sheazy I do, bro'." Also: Used as "Off the

heazy, fo' sheazy." ("Off the hook, for sure.") Also: Used as "Fo' Shizzel, my nizzel." ("For sure, my friend.") [*Origin*, African American; poeticized change on "sure"]

**Fo' sho** (foe show) *adv.*, For sure, certainly, absolutely. "Do I want to go to the movies? Fo' sho'!" [*Origin*, African American]

**Folks** (fokes) *n.*, Family members; close friends or associates. "We were folks a long time ago until she went bad." [*Origin*, African American]

**Foolio** (FU-lee-o) *n.*, A fool, a jerk, a stupid person. "What are you trying to do, foolio?" [*Origin*, 90s youth, mixture of fool and Coolio] Also: **Fool.** Originally used as disrespectful appellation but now just a term for anyone you are talking to, often a friend.

**Forty** (FOR-tee) *n.*, A forty-ounce bottle of malt liquor that has a higher alcohol concentration than beer. "After drinking a whole forty, the girl fell out." [*Origin*, '90s youth culture]

**Four-one-one, 411** (four one one) *n.*, Necessary information "Give me the 411 on that boy." [*Origin*, '90s youth culture]

**Fowl** (fowl) *adj.*, Unacceptable, unfair, not cool. "Yo, man, that kind of move is fowl." "Don't get fowl on me." [*Origin*, '70s youth]

**Freak** (FREEK) *n.*, A person who acts wild or weird; sexual activity. "He was a big freak." "It's time to get my freak on." [*Origin*, African American]

**Freaky deaky** (FREE-kee DEE-kee) *adj.,* Acting crazy or weird in a sensual way. "He was being freaky deaky." See: Freak. [*Origin,* '80s funk]

**Fresh** (fresh) *adj.,* Great, neat, cool. "That's fresh." [*Origin,* Originated by Fantastic Grand Wizard Theodore and the 5 MC's, 1978]

**Front** (fruh-nt) *v.,* Acting fake, putting on a cover. "Don't front like you're prep when you're really gangster." [*Origin,* African American]

**G** (gee) *n.,* A thousand dollars; a gang. "He's a real G." "My gramps has been kickin' down a G to me every semester." Also: Friend, comrade, member of the same gang. "Come on, G, let's get out of here." See: O.G. [*Origin,* African American]

**Gaffle** (GAF-ful) *v.,* (*past part.,* **gaffled**) Steal. "He gaffled that skrill from his mom." [*Origin,* African American]

**Game** (gaem) *n.,* Words used to attract the opposite sex through conversation, seductive speaking skill. "You ain't got no game." "I was spittin' my game when my moms called on my cell phone." [*Origin,* Hip hop]

**Gandish** (GAN-dish) *adj.,* Something not to one's likes. "This beat is pretty gandish." [*Origin,* Hindi, gandish, distasteful]

**Ganja** (GAN-ja) *n.*, Marijuana, *bot.*, cannabis sativa. "Stop dwellin' on that ganja." [*Origin,* Hindi]

ganja

**Gank** (gank) *v.*, (*past part.*, **ganked**) Steal. "He ganked the test answers from the teacher's desk." [*Origin,* African American]

**Ghetto** (GET-o) *adj.*, Broken down, cheap, worn out. "Your shoes are so ghetto." [*Origin,* From ghetto meaning African American community, considered to have less wealth; from ghetto meaning restricted Jewish districts of European cities; from Italian for the waterworks district of Venice which was a Jewish community in the middle ages.] *Usage note:* While ghetto is used widely by African American and other young people, it has a negative connotation as part of a culture of disrespect and contempt for African American working class people.

**Ghetto-fabulous** (GET-o FAB-u-lus) *adj.*, Extremely good, excellent, outstanding. "That new outfit your mom got you is ghetto-fabulous." [*Origin,* Hip hop]

**Ghost** (GOAST) *v.*, To leave the premises, to vacate, to go away. "One more dance, then I'm going to ghost." Also: Swayze, from Patrick Swayze who starred in

*Ghost.* "One more dance, then I'm going to Swayze."

**Good ol'** (gud ol) *adj.,* Sarcastic description of anything, saying it is positive but really meaning negative. "It's time for good ol' math." [*Origin,* '90s youth culture]

**Gooey balls** (GU-ee balz) *n.,* A confection, such as Rice Krispie treats, made with marijuana or hashish. "The gooey balls at Reggae on the River were only a dollar." [*Origin,* Drug subculture]

**Goth** (goth) *n.,* A person who dresses in black, sometimes with black makeup, and shows interest in things medieval, sometimes morbid. "It seems like all the Goths are growing older and leaving the scene." [*Origin,* '90s youth culture, from Gothic] See: Kinder Bat.

**Grill** (gril) *n.,* Front teeth; the full mouthful of teeth. Often used when one puts a gold apparatus on the teeth. "Man, check out how his grill is bling blingin'." [*Origin,* African American]

grill

**Grub** (grub) *v.*, To eat. Also: *n.*, Food. "Yo, everyone into the dining room, time to grub!" "I'm hungry, let's go get some grub." [*Origin*, African American]

**Grungy** (GRUN-jee) *adj.*, Filthy, grimy, soiled, unkempt. "The park is so grungy." [*Origin*, Description of dress of musicians in Seattle area in '80s punk garage bands]

**Guey** (way) *n.*, Bastard, fool. Demeaning but used often with affection. "OK, guey, I'll see you later." [*Origin*, Chicano/Spanish]

**G-unit** (Gee u-nit) *n.*, A big butt (usually female). "She got a G-unit."

grub

**Hater** (HAY-tur) *adj.*, Also: **Hatin'** (*v.*, **hating**) Someone who is against a class or group of people, someone guilty of stereotyping. "I can't stand all those playa haters." [*Origin,* African American]

**Hateration** (HAY-ter-a-shun) *n*, Hatred, dislike of people. [*Origin,* song Mary J. Blige]. Cf. worriation: "Jerry don't worry about no puzzles a-tall. Worriation ain't no part of his nature." From *The Sweet Flypaper of Life,* by Langston Hughes, 1955.

**Hatnin',** (HAT-nin) *v. pres. part.,* Happening, going on. "Hey, blood, what's hatnin'." [*Origin,* African American]

**Heat** (heet) *n.,* The police. Also: A weapon. "When the heat rolls up, you have to fade." "He's bringing the heat." [*Origin,* African American]

**Heazy** (HEE-zee) *n.,* Hook, in the phrase, "off the heazy." It means something that is "off the hook," is very good. See: Fo' sheazy. [*Origin,* African American]

**Hecka** (HEK-ah) *adv.,* Very, extremely. Grammar school variation of "hella." "That's a hecka fresh ride!" Also: **Hecksa.** (Variation: Heck-city. "That's heck-city good!") [*Origin,* Berkeley]

**Heify,** also **Hyphy** (HI fee) *adj.,* Angry, agitated. When somebody lets their adrenaline pump them up too much, they go off or get loud and crazy, uncontrollable, sometimes they even "snap." "She got all heify right in the middle of English class."

**Hella** (HEL-ah) *adv.,* Very, extremely, in large quantity. "There's hella candy in the cabinet." "That girl is hella fine." "That jacket is hella clean." Also: **Helluv** [*Origin,* Combination of "hell" and "of," Berkeley]

**Hit** (hit) *v.,* To have sexual relations. "Hey, let's hit it." Also: How much something costs. "Those shoes hit me about 180 bucks" Also: Hit that shit, to do something no one else will do, e.g., pull your pants down in a basketball game. "Hit that shit, blood!" [*Origin,* African American]

**Holla** (HOL a) *v.,* To get information from someone. "Holla at me about that girl Salina." Also, to speak to someone romantically. "Yo, girl, can I holla at you for a second?" [*Origin,* Hip Hop]

**Homie** (HO-mee) *n.,* Friend, pal, someone from the same home or neighborhood. "How ya doin', homie?" (Variation: Homes, home slice, home skillet) [*Origin,* African American]

**Hoochie** (HOO-chee) *n.,* (*adj.,* **hoochie, hoochified**) A young woman who dresses in tight clothing and wears large amounts of make-up. "She's trying to really look like a hoochie." As an adjective, can mean slutty, tacky. "That shirt is so hoochie." [*Origin,* First used in "Hoochie mama" from 2 Live Crew, hip hop] *Usage note:* Many people feel that hoochie has transcended its negative connotation and that it is also racist to identify all women who dress a certain way as a hoochie in the negative sense as this applies to many Chicano/Latino and African American female styles. They also argue that hoochie can be a state of mind, a personal statement of working class identity, or a choice of friends.

**Hood rat** (hood rat) *n.,* Literally a person who sits on the hood of the car. A young woman who dresses in teased and hair-sprayed hair, black leather, tight clothes. See: hoochie. [*Origin,* Hip hop]

**Hook, Off the hook** (HUK) *adj.,* Something that's very good. "I had so much fun at the party, it was off the hook." [*Origin,* Hip Hop]

**Hooptie** (HOOP-tee) *n.,* Old, wrecked automobile. "Let's go for a ride in my hooptie." [*Origin,* '70s youth]

**Hooride** (HU-ried) *v.,* (Also: **Hoorider, hoorode, hoorided**) To put down, destroy, ridicule. "Let's go hooride the party." "You've been hoorode." [*Origin,* African American]

hooptie

**Hot** (hot) *adj.*, Stolen, as in merchandise. "That CD player is hot, bro'." [*Origin*, '50s American]

**Hots** (hots) *n.*, Feeling of attraction, "It's so obvious that he has the hots for her."

**Hottie** (HOT-ee) *n.*, A young woman or man who is very.attractive. "She's a hottie." [*Origin*, Hip hop]

jankity

# I

**I'm cool** (im kool) *phrase,* Meaning "don't count me in." "She said she wanted to give him my number, and I said, I'm cool." [*Origin,* Hip hop]

**I'm down** (im down) *phrase,* Meaning "count me in." "If everyone wants to go there, I'm down." [*Origin,* Hip hop]

# J

**Jabronie** (ja-BROE-nee) *n.,* A stupid, weak person. "Get up, ya big jabronie." [*Origin,* Wrestling]

**Jack** (jak) *v.,* To steal "She jacked a candy bar from the grocery store." [*Origin,* Hip hop]

**Jake** (jake) *adj.,* Everything is going well. "I got the money and the car, everything's jake." [*Origin,* '40s African American]

**Jank** (jank) *v., (past part.,* **janked**) Steal. "I janked this gum from Walgreen's." [*Origin,* African American]

**Jankity** (JAN-ki-tee) *adj.,* (Also: **Janky, janked, jankity-ass, jankity-assed**) In bad shape, broken, old, in disrepair, messed up. "Her old backpack was hecka jankity." "I've got a jankity TI-82." [*Origin, African American*]

**Jargon** (JAR-gon) *n.*, Confusion. "Don't look at me, that's jargon." [*Origin, '90s youth culture*]

**Jimmy** (JI-mee) *n.*, A condom. "You'd better make sure you have a jimmy." [*Origin, Hip hop*]

**Jobber** (JAH-bur) *n.*, Someone whose only reason for being someplace, especially in the ring, is to draw attention to the fan favorite. "Al Snow is such a jobber." [*Origin, Wrestling*]

**Jock** (jahk) *v.*, To like, care for, have a crush on, flirt with. "She really jocks you." [*Origin, '90s youth culture*]

**Joint** (joynt) *n.*, A marijuana cigarette. "He rolled a joint." [*Origin, '30s drug subculture*]

**Jones** (jonz) *n.*, The craving for drugs, especially heroin. Also: Used for craving for other things. *v.*, To crave drugs. "I've got a jones for chocolate tonight." "He's really jonsin'" [*Origin, '60s drug subculture*]

**Juice** (joos) *n.*, Alcohol. "Let's get some juice and have a party." Also: *n.*, **Juicer,** an alcoholic. Also: *v. past part.*, **Juiced,** excited, anticipatory, "I'm so

juice

juiced for the game that I can hardly concentrate on homework." [*Origin*, '50s African American]

**Juvie** (JEW-vee) *n.*, Juvenile hall. "After the fight, two of them got taken out to juvie." [*Origin*, '60s youth culture]

**Key** (kee) *adj., n.*, The best, good. "I gotta say, Sublime is key." [*Origin*, '90s youth culture]

**Keyed** (keed) *v. past part.*, Drunk or high. "At the rave, we were all keyed." [*Origin*, '90s youth culture]

**Kicks** (kiks) *n.*, Shoes. "I was feeling mighty light in my new kicks." [*Origin*, '90s youth culture]

**Kinder Bat** (KIN-dur bat) *n.*, A person new to the Goth scene, a partial Goth. "I'm seeing a lot of new Kinder Bats at the *Rocky Horror Picture Show*." [*Origin*, '90s youth culture, from German kinder, child; child-bat] See: Goth.

**Knock** (NOK) *v.* (*pres. part.*, **knockin'**) Sweet, fine, beautiful, awesome. "Man, that old Mustang is really

kicks

knockin.'" Also used concerning music: "Damn, this song knocks." [*Origin,* '90s youth culture]

**Kvetch** (ka-vetch) *v.,* To complain, especially in an annoying or nagging way. "Why do you kvetch and kvetch?" Also: *n.,* Complainer, whiner. "She is such a kvetch." [*Origin,* Yiddish]

**L's** (ells) *n.,* License to drive a car. "Yo, I finally got my L's." [*Origin,* '90s youth culture]

**Lace** (layce) *v.,* To give, donate, provide. "We went out to lunch and my teacher laced me with a sandwich." [*Origin,* from Latin laqueus, noose, and lacere, to entice; used to refer to adding liquor to a drink]

**Light weight** (lite wait) *adv.,* A little bit, slightly, not entirely. "How was that party?" "Eh, it was light weight cool." Can be used as single word: "Do you like him?" "Lightweight."

**Like** (like) *prep.,* Similar to, approximately. "We lived like kings." Also: Used as a marker, space-maker in sentences—the way um and ah are used, as well as the Spanish "digo." "I'm like telling my mom that like I have to go the mall and like she's like tweakin'" [*Origin,* In this usage, first used by jazz musicians in '30s and '40s, beatniks in the '50s, youth in '60s to

now; also prominent in "valley talk"]
**Louie** (LOO-ee) *n.,* Left, as in, "The club's over that way! Hang a louie." [*Origin,* '50s beatnik slang]

**Mac** (mak) *n.,* (also spelled mack) A male who is able to get with many women. "That guy in those fancy glasses is a mac." As a verb, to be outgoing about liking someone, to flirt with skill. "He was macking her during the whole evening and never left her side." Also: **Mac-daddy,** *n.,* a popular male. [*Origin,* French, macineau, pimp]

**Mainy** (MAY-nee) *adj.,* Crazy or willing to do something no one else around will do. "You mainy, blood, and I don't want to get caught up in that." [*Origin,* African American]

**Marinate** (Mair-i-nate) *v.,* To chill or hang out or to reflect on something. "I'm just sittin' here, marinatin'." Or "Remember your first kiss, yes, marinate on that a while."

**Milkshake** (milk-shayk) *n.,* Sexuality "My milkshake is better than yours." [*Origin,* Hip hop, Kelis]

**Moded** (MO-ded) *v. past part.,* used as *adj.,* Being taken advantage of, being disrespected. "That was cold, brother, you got moded." [*Origin,* '90s youth culture]

**Mon** (mon) *n.,* Man, friend, comrade. "How ya doin', mon?" [*Origin,* Rastafarian]

**Monet** (mo NAY) *n.,* Someone who looks good from far away but looks bad up close. [*Origin,* from name of French impressionist]. "He was a straight Monet."

**Money** (MUH-nee) *n.,* Friend, good person. "Hey, I'll catch you later, money." Also: Anything good. "That was a great movie, it was money!" [*Origin,* African American]

**Monkey** (MUN-kee) *n.,* Butt. "Shake that Monkey!" [*Origin,* Hip hop, Too Short]

**Mota** (MOW-tah) *n.,* Marijuana, *bot.* cannabis sativa. "Hey, pass that mota." [*Origin,* Spanish, drug subculture]

**Mug** (mug) *v., (past part.,* **muggin'**) To make a face at someone, to stare at someone. "Why you always muggin' me?" *Usage note:* Muggin' can be used to call attention when someone is staring at someone else or making a strange face. In this case, the term can be used with affection, as in, "Hey, I saw you muggin' her all day." There is also something called "dirty muggin'" which is to stare at someone in a threatening way. If someone who is in a

muggin'

gang drives by, you can get shot for mugging them (making a threatening look). In tense situations, it is dangerous to simply make eye contact with anyone, which can be deemed mugging. In that case, you see the teen looking down at the ground.

**Mullet** (MULL it) *n.,* Men's haircut, short with bangs in front, long in back. '80s style. May have originated with Paul McCartney but has been traced back even to President James Polk. [*Origin,* from the look of a fish called the mullet which is well-known for its big head]

mullet

**Nah, naw** (nah, naw) *interj.,* No. A way of showing disagreement. "Nah, I don't want to." "Hell, naw." [*Origin,* '90s youth culture]

**Nasty, narsty** (NAS-tee, NARS-tee) *adj.,* Not tasteful, disgusting, sexually perverse. "I heard that girl got nasty after the prom." When used as a noun, sexual relations. "They were doin' the nasty." [*Origin,* Hip hop]

**Nigga** (NIG ga) *n.,* An African American. Most appropriately used between African American youth. Vernacular usage of the disparaging and racist term "nigger." See: *Nigger: The Strange Career of a Troublesome Word,* by Harvard professor Randall Kennedy. [*Origin,* from the 17th-century term for people from Africa, from French nègre and Spanish negro meaning "black"]

**Nizzel** (NI-zul) *n.,* Friend, brother, family, a familiar and friendly form of the term nigga. [Most appropriately used between African American youth. "You're my main nizzel." "Fo' shizzle ma nizzle" means "For sure my nigga." [*Origin,* African American]

**No Ma Mes** (No MAH mace) *phrase, interj.,* Literally,

don't suck on me (as a mother cow might say to her calf), don't bother me. "Hey, man, forget about it, no ma mes." [*Origin,* Chicano/Spanish]

**O.G.** (oh gee) *n.,* Original Gangster, a comrade of long standing, a veteran or elder. "We had to learn our ways from the OG's." [*Origin,* African American]

**On point** (ohn poynt) *adj.,* Well dressed, clean. "That guy is on point. His clothes are really nice."

**Out of pocket** (out of poh-ket) *adj.,* Inappropriate, ridiculous, wrong. "That dude trying to dance with just out of pocket."

**P. I.** (pee eye) *n.,* Personal information. "This information is strictly P. I." Also: *adj.,* "You have to promise to keep it P. I." [*Origin,* '80s youth]

**Packing** (PACK-ing) *v. pres. part.,* Carrying a weapon. "When that security guard grabbed me, I could feel he was packing." [*Origin,* African American]

**Pagal** (pu GOL) *adj.,* Crazy, wild, out of control.

"Avinash is really pagal these days." [Origin, Hindi]

**Patna** (PAT-na) *n.*, Friend, comrade. "Yo, patna, haven't seen you in weeks." [*Origin*, African American, from partner]

**Peace out** (pees aut) *interj.*, Goodbye, see you later. "Peace out, guys." Also: Simply "Peace." [*Origin*, African American]

**Peeps** (peeps) *n.*, Friends, associates. "I'm sticking with my peeps." [*Origin*, African American]

**Perky** (PER-kee) *adj.*, Possessing a thick butt with a slim figure. "That girl's pants make her look perky." [*Origin*, African American]

**Perved** (PERVD) *v. past part.*, Intoxicated, drunk. "He was perved after drinking that vodka."

**Phat** (fat) *adj.*, Good, great, tight, cool, wealthy. "The party was phat, we had so much fun." (Also: **Phatty,** used as noun or adjective; Phatty-phatty-bo-batty as adjective.) [*Origin*, 17th-century England; fat; hip hop usage from '80s; ph- spelling from 1981. According to some sources: acronym for "pretty hips and thighs"] See: Fat.

**Pigeon** (pige-un) *n.*, A young woman whose clothing is borrowed and doesn't have her own money. "He ended up going out with a pigeon."

**Pinche** (PEEN-chay) *adj.*, Damned, goddamned, "I can't get this pinche ride to start." [*Origin*, Chicano/Spanish]

**Pinner** (PIN-er) *n.*, A very small, tightly rolled, joint. "Hey,

don't just roll a pinner."
[*Origin,* Drug subculture]

**Played out** *v. past part.,* Out
of fashion, old, outdated.
"Those Doc Marten boots
are so played out."

**Player** (PLAY-er) *n.,* Also:
**Playa.** Someone who is
dating two or more people
at the same time. A pimp.
"Jordan thinks he is such
a player." [*Origin,* From
*Superfly* film, Curtis May-
field]

player

**Poke** (poke) *v.,* To have sexual relations. "Got to have
something to poke on." Also: *n.,* "I want to get my
poke in." Demeaning. [*Origin,* Hip hop]

**Pookie** (POO kee) *n.,* Pet name for your significant other.
"Come on over and sit with me, pookie." See: Boo.

**Pookie** (PU-kee) *n.,* Marijuana, *bot.,* cannabis sativa.
"Yo, fool, where's the pookie at?" [*Origin,* Drug cul-
ture]

**Poontang** (POON-tang) *n.,* Female genitals. "He can't
think of anything but poontang." Also: **Poonanny**
[*Origin,* '20s American South]

**Pooped** (poopt) *v. past part.,* Out of breath, exhausted.
"I was pooped after the long hike." [*Origin,* '60s youth
culture]

**Po-po** (poe poe) *n.,* The police. "Uh, oh, here comes the po-po." [*Origin,* African American]

**Poppin' a collar** (POP-in a CAL-er) *v. pres. part.,* A style of dancing in which the dancer holds his/her collar and rocks gently to the music. "Those hood rats are always poppin' a collar." Also used as "What's happening?" in "What's poppin'?" [*Origin,* Hip hop]

**Profilin'** (PRO fie lin) *v. pres. part.,* Driving around with your friends in a scraper, playing loud music, trying to get others to notice how fine you are. "I know he was out profilin' last night!" [*Origin,* Hip hop]

**Props** (props) *n.,* Respect, credit that is due to one, credit for accomplishment. "I've gotta give props to the teachers we had." [*Origin,* Hip hop]

**Psych** (SIKE) *v.,* Playing mind games, confusing and dominating the other person. From psychology. Also used as single word expletive, declaring that someone has been tricked. "Did you catch that advertisement?" "Psyche!"

**Punk** (punk) *n.,* A person into the punk music scene; a coward; someone who deliberately attempts to annoy. "I knew he'd turn out to be a punk." [*Origin,* '80s youth]

**Rapstar** (RAP-star) *n.*, A man who doesn't have a main girlfriend, who talks to many different young women. See: playa. Also: Rapstar status. "He is starting to act like a rapstar all the time." [*Origin*, African American]

**Ras** (ras) *interj.*, An exclamation of surprise. "Ras, you scared me there!" [*Origin*, Rastafarian]

**Rat Head** (rat hed) *n.*, Low class person, usually a female, who carries herself in an inappropriate way or dresses trashy. "Oh, no, those braids need to come out, she is such a rat head." [*Origin*, African American]

**Reachin'** (REECH-in) *v. pres. part.*, Ready to fight. "If she says that shit again, I'll be reachin' for her." [*Origin*, African American]

**Real talk** (reel tawk) *n.*, Serious talk, not joking around. "Real talk, where are we going tonight." [*Origin*, '90s youth culture]

**Represent** (re-pree-SENT) *v.*, To make a good showing; to stand up for, to be role model, to give respect to. "I don't care where you started out from, now that you're here you've got to represent." [*Origin*, African American]

**Rigoddamnediculous** (ree-god-dam-DI-ku-luss) *adj.*,

Grossly negative, highly irregular, superbly interesting. An expression used to hyperbolically explain the magnitude of an event, comment, action, belief, etc., in its abnormality. "The fact that an idiot is president is rigoddamnediculous." Cf. Absofuckinglutely [*Origin*, '90s youth culture]

**Rippa', Ripper** (RIP-a) *n.*, A girl who is wild and may be having sex with more than one person or with multiple partners. "That girl is a rippa'." [*Origin*, African American]

**Rollers** (ROLL-erz) *n.*, The police. "Duck down, here come the rollers." [*Origin*, African American]

**Rollin'** (ROL-in) *v. pres. part.*, Driving in a car. On a drug, usually ecstasy. Traveling from one place to another. Making a marijuana joint with your hands. "Yo, I'm rollin' like a mad man." Rollin' deep: traveling with a larger group or crew. [*Origin*, African American]

**Runner** (Runn-er) *v.*, The opposite sex of a ripper, a boy who has more than one sexual partner. "Don't mess with him, he's a runner." [*Origin*, African American]

**Saucy** (SAW-see) *adj.*, Attractive, fondly regarded, sweet. "Those new shoes are hella saucy." [*Origin*, African American]

**Savage** (SAV-age) *adj.*, To be hard core, strong, wild. "Bruce Lee is a savage!"

**Scan'lous** (SCAN-lus) *adj.*, From scandalous. Especially mean, evil, and cold-hearted. "That vice principal was scan'lous the way he picked on our group." Also: **Scandocious** (scan-DOSH-us) [*Origin*, African American, E-40 lyrics]

**Schmabbin'** (SCHMA-bin) *v. pres. part.*, Driving fast, burning tire rubber when starting out. Peeling out. Also: Driving around in the car with a group of friends, playing the radio loud, shouting out. "Yeah, we were straight schmabbin' last night." [*Origin*, '90s youth culture]

**Schmank** (shmank) *interj.*, An exclamation to show distress or unhappiness. "Schmank! Did you hear that prom tickets are sold out already!" [*Origin*, '90s youth culture]

**Schmutz** (shmutz) *n.*, A bit of food or dirt, usually on the face. "You have a little schmutz on your lip." [*Origin*, Yiddish]

**Scrape** (scraype) *v.*, To beat up, to whoop somebody. "He was out of pocket so I jumped in and scraped him." [*Origin,* African American]

**Scraper** (SCRAP ur) *n.*, An old school car, usually a Buick. Often fixed up with fancy, loud stereo systems. "Coach Malik's baby blue scraper got slap!" [*Origin,* African American]

**Scratch** (skrach) *n.*, Money, cash. "Do me a favor and gimme some scratch until tomorrow." [*Origin,* African American]

**Scrub** (skrub) *n.*, A person who is a loser or makes a fool of himself. *v.* to fall or fail in some way. "That fool was such a scrub, I had to let him go." "I dribbled the ball down the court just fine and then I scrubbed just before the buzzer." [*Origin,* TLC song]

**Scuffed** (skuft) *adj.*, (*past part. of verb* scuff) Beat up, messed up, or ugly. "I came out of that party looking really scuffed." [*Origin,* African American]

**Served** (survd) *v. past part.*, To be put down or beat up. "You got served!" [*Origin,* basketball slang]

**Set** (set) *n.*, A group of friends. "We're going to let her hang out with our set this weekend." [*Origin,* African American]

**Shady** (SHAY-dee) *adj.*, Mean, unfair, untrustworthy, dishonest. "These small town police are shady." [*Origin,* African American] See: Shisty.

**Shake** (shayke) *n.*, The less desirable parts of the marijuana plant, that which is left over, shaken onto the table, after the best part, the buds, have been taken out. "Hey, I can just give you some of this shake." See: Bammer. [*Origin,* Drug subculture]

**Shiggity** (shigidy) *adv.,* For sure, positively. "Are you going to be at the concert tonight?" "Oh, fo shiggity!" [*Origin,* poeticized change on "sure"]

**Shiselal** (SHI-ze-lal) *n.,* Stuff, goods, credit. "Man, help me out with some shiselal." [*Origin,* '90s youth culture]

**Shisty** (SHY-stee) *adj.,* Mean, dishonest, scandalous. "That guy is acting hella shisty." [*Origin,* African American] See: Shady.

**Shorty** (SHOR-tee) *n.,* Girlfriend. "I have the sweetest shorty." [*Origin,* African American]

**Shotgun, Shotti** (SHOT-gun, SHOT-ee) *n.,* The front right passenger seat. "I called shotgun so I could pick the radio stations." [*Origin,* Old West, stagecoach movies]

**Sick** (sik) *adj.,* Good or bad, depending on the context. "Check out that outfit ... it's sick." "Oh man, that track is so sick!" Also: **Ill.** Extremely deep and profound. "That new rapper is hella ill." [*Origin,* African American]

**Skank** (skank) *n.,* Someone

shotgun

who is easily accessible sexually or behaves like a prostitute, a shallow person. "I can't believe that she got with him. She is such a skank!" Also: **Skanky**, *adj.*, Disgusting, unappealing, dirty. [*Origin*, Hip hop]

**Skeevy** (SKEE-vee) *adj.*, Slimy, inappropriate "That skeevy guy over there is your boyfriend!?" [*Origin*, African American]

**Skittle** (SKIT-tul) *n.*, One who is of multi-racial ancestry and or appears to be so by skin color. Used primarily by females of white and black descent. "Sadie is one of my favorite skittles." [*Origin*, African American]

**Skrill, Skrilla** (skrill, SKRIL-a) *n.*, Money, cash. "I can't go out unless I get some skrill." [*Origin*, Berkeley High]

**Slang** (slang) *v.*, (*pres. part.*, **Slangin'**) Variation on sling, slinging. To sell drugs, especially cocaine, especially on the street. "His brother is gonna go down, he's steady slangin' outside the apartments." [*Origin*, African American]

**Slap** (SLAP) *n.*, Something that is happening, tight, or pleasing to young people. "That song got slap!" As a verb: "He was slappin' his music so hard that his headphones blew out!" See: Knock.

**Soldier** (sold-gher) *n.*, A person who is down, who stands up for himself or herself. "You my patna', you my soldier. For reals." [*Origin*, Street Soldiers, radio program of the S.F. Omega Boys Club; and Sister

Soulja, hip hop philosopher and writer, *The Coldest Winter Ever*]

**Spew** (spew) *v.,* To vomit or throw up. "Sorry I spewed on your carpet." Also: **Hurl** [*Origin,* '80s youth culture; also inspired by Mike Myers and Dana Carvey in the movie *Wayne's World*]

**Spinna, Sprees** (spinner, sprees) *n.,* Wheel hubcaps that keep turning when the car stops, using both an inner and an outer rim. "Look at Damien's new spinnas!"

**Sprung** (sprung) *adj.,* To be seriously attracted to someone "He was sprung off her." [*Origin,* Hip hop]

**Stagin'** (STAJ-in) *v. pres. part.,* Showing someone off, putting someone in the spotlight, usually in front of a crowd. "Yvette, let me see your homework." "Yo, teach, stop stagin' me in front of the whole class." Also: **Front street,** as in, "Thanks a lot for puttin' me on front street." [*Origin,* African American]

**Stomp it out** (Staump it out) *phrase,* To dance, stomping the ground. "When the music comes on, I'm 'bout to stomp it out." [*Origin,* African American]

**Stoned** (stond) *v. past part.,* High on drugs. [*Origin,* Ray Charles "Let's go get stoned."]

**Stoner** (STO-nur) *n.,* A person who uses drugs habitually. A person who smokes marijuana often. "I don't hang out with him anymore, he's such a stoner." [*Origin,* '60s youth culture. Ray Charles's "Let's Go Get Stoned;" Bob Dylan's "Everybody Must Get Stoned"]

**Straight (up)** (strayt up) *adv.,* Truthfully, absolutely.

"She straight up told me she likes that boy." [*Origin,* Hip hop]

**Strapped** (strapt) *v. past part.,* Carrying a weapon. "When Shaft went underground, he was always strapped." [*Origin,* African American]

**Stuntin'** (STUN-tin) *v. pres. part.,* Wearing expensive clothes and jewels to show that you have money to waste. "He's always stuntin' when he shows at the dance." [*Origin,* African American]

**Stupid** (stoopid) *adj.,* Also: Dumb, a loose style of dance. Go stupid: a type of dance where you shake your head from side to side and move your body (stupidly). "I went to the party and everyone went stupid." [*Origin,* African American]

**Suck** (suk) *v.,* To be bad, negative, hateful. "This school really sucks." [*Origin,* '70s youth culture; in modern usage, no sexual connotation]

**Swanson** (SWAN-sun) *n.,* Coward, one who will back down when confronted. "What a swanson." [*Origin,* African American]

**Swear** (sware) *interj.,* Used similar to "oh no," or "that's not true, is it?" or just "holy cow!" "Steve is going out with Betty now." "Swear!"

**Swerve** (swerv) *n.,* Drunkenness. "I've gotta get my swerve on." As *verb, past part.,* swerved. "That guy is hella swerved, don't let him drive." [*Origin,* '90s youth culture]

**Swolles** (swolz) *n.,* Muscles, from swollen. "That guy has some hella big swolles." [*Origin*, African American]

**Swoop** (swoop) *v.*, To pick up, to meet up with. "I'll swoop you at about 9 tonight!" Also, a hairstyle in which the hair is parted on one side and brushed over the eye on the other side. "For prom, I want a swoop in my hair." [*Origin*, '90s youth culture]

swerved

# T

**Tacked** (takt) *v. past part.,* (Also: **Tact, taxed**) Drunk or high. "That boy who never comes to class is always tacked." [*Origin,* Drug subculture]

**Tag** (tag) *v.,* To write an inscription on a wall using spray paint, to put up graffiti. Also used as noun, the writing one has put on the wall, or the signature of the artist. "He knew that was my tag up there on the bridge overpass." "We almost got busted by the police when we were out tagging last night." [*Origin,* Hip Hop]

**Talk to** (tahk to) *v.,* To go out with or date someone. "Are you talking to Ashley?"

tag

**Thang** (thang) *n.,* A thing. Attractive item. "There are all kinds of thangs I want for Christmas." [*Origin,* African American]

**Thick** (thik) *adj.,* Description of a woman with big breasts and large booty. Not skinny. "She's got it goin' on, she's thick." [*Origin,* African American]

**Throw up (a tag)** (throw-up) *v.,* To write an inscription on a wall using spray paint, to put up graffiti.

**Tight** (tite) *adj.,* Good, cool, striking, appealing, trendy, great, amazing. "Your calculator is so tight." "My New Year's Eve was tight." Also: *interj.,* Great, wonderful. "We're heading out to the store for more food. Tight!" Also: **Tighty whities,** jockey underwear. [*Origin,* Hip hop]

**To'** (toe) *n.,* Also: **To' up.** From, torn up. Disheveled, messed up, dirty, in disarray or disorder. "That guy was to'." Used in: To' up from the flo' up ("Torn up from the floor up.)" and To' back (meaning "messed up.") [*Origin,* African American]

**Toot** (toot) *n.,* Prostitute. "Sometimes you act like such a toot." [*Origin,* African American]

**Trillin'** (TRIL-in) *adj.,* Relaxing or chillin' with friends, sometimes while intoxicated. A combination to trippin' and chillin'. "My friends and I were just trillin' last night." [*Origin,* '90s youth culture]

**Trippin'** (TRI-pin) *v. pres part.,* To be overly upset, overly concerned. "Man, there was no need to smash the mirror. That fool is trippin'!"

**Tuch** (tuch) *v.*, To express anger, condemnation. "Tuch you, man." [*Origin*, '90s youth culture]

**Turkey bacon** (turkee bayk-on) *n.*, Undercover police. "Put that away, I think those guys are turkey bacon." [*Origin*, Berkeley]

**Tweaker** (TWEE-kur) *n.*, An unusual person, someone who acts weird, someone who worries extensively. A drug addict. "Look at all those tweakers kickin' it in the park!" Also: *v.*, To worry too much. "Stop tweakin', mom, I can bring the grade up by the semester reports." [*Origin*, Hip hop]

**Twenty-four-seven, 24/7** (24-7) *adv.*, All the time, constantly. "My friend and I talk on the phone 24/7." [*Origin*, '90s youth culture]

twenty-four-seven

**Twerkin'** (TWUR kin) *v. pres. part.*, Dancing in sexually suggestive manner. "He was really twerkin' on the floor." [*Origin*, Hip Hop]

**Twomp** (twamp) *n.*, Twenty. Also: Twenty dollars, often referring to a quantity of marijuana. "Can I borrow a twomp?" "I got me a twomp sack." [*Origin*, Hip hop]

**Victorbaron** (vik-tur-BAR-un) *n.,* Marijuana, *bot.* cannabis sativa. "You take away my victorbaron and you'll be violatin' my civil rights." [*Origin,* Drug subculture]

**Wack** (wak) *adj.,* Bad, negative, messed up, terrible. "That new CD from Britney Spears is wack." Superlative form is: wickity-wack, something especially bad, negative, terrible. "That one from Christina Aguilera is wickity-wack. [*Origin,* African American]

**Wannabe** (WAN-a-bee) *n., adj.,* Someone who "wants to be" something he/she isn't, such as an athlete, a strong person, a leader. "That Eddie is such a wannabe." "Yeah, he's a wannabe rock star." [*Origin,* African American]

**Wazzup** (waz-ZUP) *interj.,* What's up? What's happening? How are you doing? Variation: wazzupers? "Hello? Oh, hi, wazzup?" [*Origin,* '90s youth culture]

**Whip** (wip) *n.,* Automobile, car. "The whips in his driveway were so clean!

**Whoady** (WHOE-dee) *n.*, Friend, family. "He's been my whoady for three years." [*Origin*, New Orleans]

**WOM** (wom) *n.*, Woman over man, a guy who chooses his significant other over his friends. "We asked him to go to the game with us but he couldn't go, had to hang out with his girlfriend. He's such a WOM." [*Origin*, Berkeley]

**Womp** (wahmp) *v.*, To be negative, sometimes to smell bad. "This sucks, this really womps." [*Origin*, Berkeley High]

**Word** (werd) *interj.*, An exclamation of agreement, affirmation. Also: **Word up.** "That's the best jump shot I've ever seen!" "Word!" [*Origin*, '60s African American, church]

**Yo** (yo) *interj.*, Can replace Hey or What's up? "Yo, what are you doing after school?" [*Origin*, Hip Hop]

**Yoink** (yoink) *exclam.*, Used while stealing something quickly. "I think I like your cat ... yoink!" [*Origin*, *The Simpsons*, 1990]

yoink

**Zuke** (zook) *n.*, A man dressed in Latin style, very stylishly and carefully dressed. A Chicano/Latino male. "Man, that guy was a real zuke." [*Origin,* Chicano/Spanish]

The following students contributed to the *Berkeley High School Slang Dictionary:*

| | |
|---|---|
| Sonia Abrams | Chinaka Hodge |
| Natalia Ackley-Barahona | Alex Hoff |
| Sophia Alderman | Boomer Hurwitz |
| Germey Baird | Adia Imara |
| Aramon Bartholomew | Brian Jackson |
| Charlie Benton | Julian James |
| Hemant Bhakta | Brittenee Johnson |
| Hemini Bhakta | Martín Juarez |
| Portia Boni | Georgia Kellogg |
| Andrea Braasch | Sophie Kreiss |
| Morgan Bryant | Simon Leaver-Appelman |
| Makenda Burroughs-Miller | Jared Lee |
| | Joanna Letz |
| Charles R. Carter | Peter Letz |
| Rafael Casal | Dan Levine |
| Lola Chenyek | Dani Levy |
| Zachary Cohen | Ainye Long |
| Jonah Cohn | Jeffrey Lu |
| Sophia Cohn | Victoria Maldonado |
| Lee Coleman | Lando Martinez-Greene |
| Brandon Crowder | Maeven McGovern |
| Nadji Dawkins | Beth Midanik-Blum |
| Chandrika Francis | Greg Mitchell |
| Robyn Ganeles | Salita Mitchell |
| Calvin Gaskin | Veronica Muñoz |
| Mayyan Geller | Nicholas Pace |
| Haben Godefa | Deepak Paul |
| Sam Hammer-Nahman | Yvette Perez |
| John Hargis | Darryl Perkins |

Ben Petrofsky
Max Piha
Nina Quiñones
Aja Range
Matthew Reiter
Courtney Richardson
Tanisha Robinson
Jesse Roll-Beyea
Rebecca Rozo-Marsh
Luis Rubio
Josh Sabbah
Ferron Salniker
Lizbeth Sanders
Daniel Schindelman-Schoen
Daniel Silber-Baker
David Silber-Baker
Nathan Simmons
Nikki Sonfield
Séla Steiger
Ahimsa Stone
Tirharqa Stone
Chayla Summers
Simon Trabelsi
Spenser Veale
Maria Wahlstrom
Katy Wiggins
David Woodard
Kenneth Wycoff